IT'S YOUR SEASON

STEPS TO A MORE EXCELLENT LIFE RIGHT NOW

Nicole Thornton

ISBN 978-1-63903-732-2 (paperback)
ISBN 978-1-63903-733-9 (digital)

Christian Faith Publishing
832 Park Avenue
Meadville, PA 16335
www.christianfaithpublishing.com

Printed in the United States of America

ACKNOWLEDGMENTS

I'd like to take this opportunity to first thank God for all that He has done, is doing, and will be doing in my life; for without God I am nothing. I'd like to also thank my behind the scene supporters for their words of encouragement and financial contribution in helping me to put this divine assignment together. I give thanks to Linda Nevith, Minter "Chucky" Cluff, Aunt Marcella Plummer, and Cheryl Leftridge. Thank you so much for all of your support and for keeping the writing of this book in the strictness of confidence. Words cannot express how much your support means to me.

I'd also like to take this time to acknowledge my grandmother, Lucille Dace, whose voice I continue to hear in my ear, even though she has been called home to be with the Lord for 8 years now. She said to me, "Baby I love you, I really do and I thank God for you." She then would say, "Remember you can do anything you set your mind to. Some people think their way out of doing things, like me, but you think about it and you do it." I just wish I had set my mind to have done more sooner. I dedicate this book to her, my grandmother Lucille Dace. Thank you grandma for your words of wisdom and encouragement. God allowed me to see you live well into your 103rd year and you are truly missed, however never forgotten. Love you grandma!

CHAPTER 1

BE FED UP

Nothing happens until you're fed up with your current situation.

Do you consider yourself to be sincerely happy and do you feel accomplished in life? Do you wake up in the morning excited about the day ahead? Do you feel a sense of fulfillment, and are you looking forward to getting to your place of employment in the morning? Do you feel that you are living in your purpose, or are you desperately trying to discover what your purpose is as you are just going through the motions? Do you feel as if there has to be more to life?

As we get into the following pages, we will look at different ways to obtain the life we were created for. We'll take a look at different suggestions to help anyone live a happier and more fulfilled life, something we all should want and certainly something we all should have.

Many people already have a sense of satisfaction and may feel they are already serving their purpose. I applaud them, good for them. Life is so much better for the individual and the people around them when purpose is being lived out. This book is for those who are hungry for more and not quite sure where to start on that journey. In perspective, one should never feel as though there's no room for greater achievements and growth. There are those who are totally complacent with where they are in life. They have no desire for anything more. Yes, we should be content; however, we should never find ourselves being complacent. Setting goals and having visions and improvements is what should be the driving force for continuous growth. However, this self-help book is designed for those who know there's more out there for their lives but are just not sure how to go about getting it.

Let me start by saying nothing will ever begin to change until you obtain the attitude of being fed up and tired of the same mediocre life you've created for yourself. We should be wanting more out of our current life, situation, career, education, relationships, so on and so forth. If you're not uncomfortable enough with your current life and lifestyle, you will not want to make any changes. Therefore, being uncomfortable and fed up along with determination for more, is what will help us strive for change. It's not the only thing needed, but without a desire for change, most likely you'll remain in your current position in life.

Many people live day-to-day doing whatever it is they do and doing it well and very comfortably. Some are actually feeling happy and fulfilled. Then there's those who feel as if there's so much more to obtain in life, as though they are not living out their full potential. Some feel as if they are just here on earth going through the motions and may even feel like they are on some kind of a treadmill in life to some degree. Always moving and moving fast, but never getting anywhere. Most people know that there's more but are not exactly sure on what it is they want and certainly don't know how to go about obtaining what it is we want.

Trust me, I totally understand. For so long I've felt as if I could be doing more and should be doing more but never truly knew what exactly. Sometimes, the frustration of not knowing how to go about going after more keeps us right where we are, right in our familiar place where comfort often accompanies that. We find all kinds of excuses why we shouldn't make moves rather than reasons we should. We have to refuse to allow our limiting beliefs and fear keep us from moving towards our goals. Fear of failure will keep us stagnant. We'll talk more about fear and limiting beliefs later.

Most people don't handle change well, I can attest to that. However, it is often said, if you want something different, you have to do something different.

Another familiar statement by Albert Einstein is, "The definition of insanity is doing the same thing over and over again but expecting different results."

I remember talking to a random woman in the airport while I was traveling to another country as she kept speaking, she went on to say how she missed her flight earlier. I then responded, "Wow, I've missed a flight once in my life, and I was actually in the airport hours in advance." I finished up saying with the statement, "I'd rather be in the airport waiting at the gate in peace rather than being on the road with anxiety thinking that I'm going to miss my flight."

She went on to explain to me that she has missed fourteen flights that she can recall. I looked at her in amazement and my jaw dropped, and I thought how in the world does one do that, but I said out loud, "Fourteen flights?" She then replied, "Yes, fourteen," as she's nodding her head. I was actually confused. I then said, "Wow, how do you miss fourteen flights?" She then responded, saying that she never leaves the house early enough. All I could say was, "Wow!" With a shocked look on my face. I had the nerve to continue to engage with this woman and asked her why wouldn't she leave her house a little earlier? She said that she lives less than an hour away making it clear that the drive is not that long. I shut my mouth and thought to myself as long as she's going to continue to do the same thing, she's going to keep missing flights. To me that was insanity.

There are many people out there that decide to take a chance on themselves by investing in themselves and stepping out of their comfort zone to do something different to obtain something different. We have the "enough is enough" attitude and can no longer sit and do nothing. Change is there waiting for us to take hold of it.

Has anyone ever told you that you missed your calling? If you are still breathing and reading this book, it's not too late. Oftentimes people can see the potential in us that we cannot see in ourselves. I encourage you to get fed up with your current situation if it's not bringing you the joy and satisfaction that you desire and the lifestyle that you dream of and let's go after that life we were created for. Let's live our purpose on purpose.

Go to www.iamlife888.com for more information and to schedule your free breakthrough call or by email at 888Iamlife@ gmail.com.

CHAPTER 2

MAKE SOME CHANGES

You cannot keep doing the same things expecting different results.

Now that we are fed up, this is the time to make some necessary changes. So you may ask, what kind of changes? Let's take a look at our environment. Do you have stress in your home? Is there stress at the job? Do you watch a lot of news, and are you constantly being updated with negative reports? How about drama on reality TV? OMG, that right there is straight ridiculous and designed to pull you right in. The fear from news updates and the drama from reality TV are straight toxicity. Are you the dumping ground for your complaining friends, or do you complain a lot yourself? Are you fearful, are you pessimistic, or are you fearlessly optimistic?

Whatever the case may be, change is possible if you want it.

See, there's so much mess that we allow into our lives that actually hinder us from growing and producing positive results in our lives. Whatever is not going to help us have a more complete, satisfying, and productive life, we need to let them go. You will get out what you put in, so we have to change what we are putting into ourselves or what we allow others to deposit in us as well.

Sometime ago, I started a technique that had me view myself as if I were a garden. I knew that whatever was planted, that's what was to be expected to grow. Therefore, I had to become very much aware of what I was planting into my life. First thing needed was to clear the ground and pull up the weeds and remove any debris such as stones and twigs out of the way in order to prepare the soil—"my heart"—to receive seeds. That means being selective on what news I was taking in and for what duration of time. Be mindful to not take part in any gossip. Also had to get rid of all bitterness and resentment as well as unforgiveness that I may have been holding on to. Had to keep my surroundings clear from people who came with drama and always found something to complain about. I became conscious of what I was letting into my soil again, "my heart."

I have to also mention we need to remove any and all negative beliefs that we have about ourselves that keep us from growing fully into the person we were created to be. Some of those beliefs have been planted in us since we were very young and many since we became older. Maybe someone made you feel you weren't smart enough, good enough, pretty enough, thin enough, and so on. These thoughts and ideas have been embedded deep into our soil "heart." Our soil has been exposed to all kinds of harsh weather and subjected to a tough environment. Low self-esteem, fear, lack of drive, and no desire have seeped into our soil and have kept us from producing better fruit.

As we prepare our soil by removing all the waste, we are able to replace and plant new seeds, new ideas, and new truths to see break ground and bud up. We start to tell ourselves we are good enough, we are smart enough, yes, we can do and be and accomplish what it is we want to achieve. We surround ourselves with people who encourage us while staying away from people who are toxic for our soil. We remind ourselves of how great we are. We find something positive in everything and in everyone. We strive to keep a positive attitude more often than not so that we are able to see the fruits of the new seeds sown.

Having a good attitude is certainly going to help us change how we enjoy life. A positive attitude is a mental attitude that sees the good and the accomplishments in your life rather than the negative and the failures. A positive attitude is a mindset that helps you see and recognize opportunities. A positive attitude means positive thinking. It is optimism and maintaining a positive mindset.

Here are some benefits of having a positive attitude:

- It helps achieve goals and attain success.
- It brings more happiness into your life.
- It produces more energy.
- Positive attitude increases your faith in your abilities and brings hope for a brighter future.
- You become able to inspire and motivate yourself and others.

- And a positive attitude allows you to have better relationships and social life.
- It increases productivity at work.
- Overcoming obstacles becomes easier.

When we have a better attitude, our speech is different.

We become more mindful of the words that come off our tongues. We tend to speak in such a way that is encouraging and uplifting to those who hear us and also to ourselves.

Some may ask, why is speech so important? Choosing to use words effectively is important in our daily lives because words have power.

Your words have an impact, so think before you speak.

Luke 6:45 (KJV) says, "For out of the abundance of his heart his mouth speaks." You will speak either positive or negative and whatever is spoken, you create more of it.

Ephesians 4:29 (NLT) says, "Don't use foul or abusive language. Let everything you say be good and helpful so that your words will be an encouragement to those who hear them."

Proverbs 18:21 (AMP) says, "Death and life or in the power of the tongue, and those who love it and indulge it will eat its fruit and bear the consequences of their words."

Below are some other necessary changes:

- Stop complaining. Nothing positive comes out of complaining. Where focus goes energy flows.

- Confucius said, "The man who chases two rabbits catches neither."

- Focus on fewer things and get really good at them.

- Declutter your life and your surroundings.

- Keep showing up.

- Do more than what's expected of you.

- Be enthusiastic.

- View problems as opportunities.

- Be grateful for what you have.

- Set up and stick to a routine.

- And don't lose hope.

The bottom line here is, if you're tired of your current situation, want more for yourself and make some changes.

Go to www.iamlife888.com for more information and to schedule your free breakthrough call or by email at <u>888Iamlife@</u> <u>gmail.com</u>.

CHAPTER 3

WHAT'S YOUR PURPOSE AND VISION

Knowing your purpose and having a vision is
like having a roadmap for your life.

Let's talk about *purpose*. So many of us live day to day not really knowing what our purpose is. We all have a purpose for our lives, and we need to know what that is.

Do you know your purpose?

What is the meaning of the word *purpose*? As a noun, it means "the reason for which something is done or created or for which something exists."

Discovering what your purpose is in life serves as a very important factor to a more successful, happier, and complete life. We are all here on this earth for a reason. God has a purpose for each and every one of us, and it's our duty and our responsibility to find out what it is and to live in it. We do ourselves and others a disservice when we are not living in our purpose. There's somebody out there who is waiting for you to show up. When we know why God has created us, we're able to overcome the challenges and the limitations of life with grace. We are not here by accident; we all have a plan for our lives so let's make a conscious decision to discover what it is that we are called to do. Some people are living a sad life because they do not know why they are here. Living a life with purpose sets you apart from others who are not.

Exodus 9:16 (NIV) says, "But I have raised you up for this very purpose, that I might show you my power and that my name might be proclaimed in all the earth."

Some benefits of knowing and living your life purpose are:

• Peace. You will have peace in your life

- Confidence. When you know your purpose you become confident because of the assurance that you are doing the right thing

- Perseverance. It's easier to persevere through obstacles you'll find along the way. Nothing can stop you from doing what God put into your heart.

Your purpose will also provide meaning to your life. And this will give you the mental tools you need to face the ups and downs in life.

Jack Canfield said, "Clarify your purpose. What is the why behind everything you do? When we know this in life, it is very empowering, and the path is clear."

One may ask, "How do I know if I'm living in my purpose now and if not? How can I find out what my purpose is?" Great questions.

Here are a few signs that you are not living in your true purpose:

1. *You don't believe you have a purpose.* Maybe you're just one of those types of people that don't buy into the notion that everyone has a purpose. We all change and influence the energy in the world, and we all have unique gifts to offer. So the truth is we all have a purpose

2. *Your big dreams are on hold.* If you believe you do have a purpose and maybe even knowing what it is, but you are putting your most inspired ideas on the back burner, most likely you are not living in it. You may worry that your dreams are just too big and unrealistic, and you tend to stay in your comfort zone but deep down inside, you know you're wasting your valuable time.

3. *Happiness doesn't last.* You'll find the things that make you happy can't keep you happy when you aren't in tune with your proper purpose.

4. *Other people dictate your life path.* We all have people in our lives who do have good intentions. Direct us to where they think we should go and what they think we should do. If we continue to do what it is they want us to do, we never really get into what is meant for us and in this case, it's our purpose. We are not living our lives; we are living their lives.

5. *You're always saying "someday."* So if for some reason you do know your purpose, but you're not actively pursuing it and always saying "someday," most likely you're saying "someday" to help make you feel better about not being in your purpose today.

6. *You have little to no energy.* People without purpose are often lethargic and tired, struggling to get up and start the day, as well as dealing with some sort of depression. This is because of a fundamental sense of restlessness that isn't being addressed as well as a lack of direction.

7. *The work you do makes you miserable.* It doesn't matter if people think you have an amazing job or career because if you are unhappy doing that, most likely you

are not living in accordance with your true purpose/ calling especially if you haven't made plans to leave that job.

Here are a few signs that you are living in your purpose:

1. Change is no longer a fear. You have learned that change is what allows you to create a lifestyle that you absolutely love.

2. You stop struggling. You live your life passionately both professionally and personally.

3. You invest in yourself and in your business. You realize the more you do the more others will invest in you and in your services.

4. You stop playing it small and you feel vibrant and alive. You realize that you have so much more to give.

5. You stop seeking approval from those around you. You have discovered your voice, courage, and confidence.

6. Work brings joy. Work is no longer sucking the energy out of your life.

7. Instead of seeking clients they are seeking you. Your income and your business are flowing.

A few ways to discover your life purpose. Remember your purpose is not something you need to make up, it's already in you. Yes, it's already there. Also, know this, it's never too late to find out what your purpose is, and no, you are not too old.

1. Explore the things you love to do and what comes easy to you (the things you're good at).
2. Ask yourself what is it that you would love to do with your life if money was not an object. I'm saying *anything at all.*
3. Ask yourself what do you do that makes you happy.
4. Surround yourself with positive people.
5. Find out what energizes you.

Regardless of where you are on your journey, discovering what your true purpose is gets you on the right path towards your more excellent life.

> For I know the plans I have for you, declares the Lord, plans for welfare and not for evil, to give you a future and a hope. (Jeremiah 29:11ESV)

> And we know that for those who love God all things work together for good, for those who are called according to his purpose. (Romans 8:28 ESV)

> You did not choose me, but I chose you and appointed you that you should go and bear fruit and that your fruit should abide, so that whatever you asked the father in my name, he may give it to you. (John 15:16 ESV)

You are not alone in this process. Let's ask ourselves the necessary questions so that we can truly discover what our purpose is, so we can do and be what we were created to do and be. You got this.

Let's talk about *vision*: again, the same as purpose, so many live day by day with no vision.

Do you have a vision?

What is the definition of vision? Vision is a practical guide for creating plans, setting goals and objectives, making decisions, and coordinating and evaluating the work on any project, large or small.

As a noun, the word *vision* means

- the faculty or state of being able to see;
- the ability to think about or plan the future with imagination or wisdom;
- a mental image of what the future will or could be like;
- an experience of seeing someone or something in a dream or trance, or as a supernatural apparition; and

- a vivid mental image, especially a fanciful one of the future.

As a verb, the word *vision* means "to imagine."

Why is it important to have a vision?

"Where there is no vision, the people perish…" (Proverbs 29:18 KJV).

1. A vision puts substance behind your goals.

It is very important to set goals for moving forward. Without establishing goals, it's more difficult to create a path to success. If you're just creating goals without a larger destination in mind, it becomes labor in vain.

Think of your vision as if it is the destination. It is your end goal. It gives you a larger purpose to outline the little goals you set along the way. Let's consider it to be your finish line.

Creating a vision puts meaning behind your goals. Instead of just hoping you end up in the right place, have a long-term destination to progressively move in the right direction.

2. Having a vision makes it easier to get through roadblocks.

When you're trying to grow as a well-rounded individual or as an entrepreneur, you're destined to run into some roadblocks. If you're not struggling, then you're not trying hard enough. But when you hit these roadblocks and hurdles, you need something that pushes you through.

That's exactly what your vision does. When you're focused on your vision, you realize just how important getting through each one of those hurdles and road-blocks are.

Set a life vision that will keep you focused. Something that will make you want to work even harder when those hurdles or tough situations arise. When you know what you're working toward, it seems like those hurdles become much smaller.

3. A vision sets your expectations

When you know your life vision, it allows you to set your expectation for success. It's been said, "great expectation is a needful thing." When you know what you want to accomplish in life, you'll know if you're getting closer to meeting your own personal expectations of success. Having a life goal can help you stay focused on your own path and not those around you.

4. Vision creates the energy and will to make change happen.

It inspires individuals and organizations to commit, to persist, and to give their best.

What's the difference between a life vision and long-term goals?

Goals are individual experiences in accomplishments you strive for. A vision is the bigger picture. Your life's vision defines what you want to be known for, who you want to be and a set of experiences and accomplishments you aim for. Your vision helps you define the goals by giving you a framework to evaluate those goals.

Your vision becomes your why. Your vision should answer questions like:

1. What do you believe you're capable of in life? What are the greatest things you could accomplish, given the right circumstances, resources, and motivation?

2. What kinds of people do you want to be surrounded by?

3. When you die, what would you want people to say and remember about you?

4. What do you wish you could change about the world? What could you contribute to the world that would make you feel proud and content?

5. What kind of life do you want to live at the ages twenty-five, thirty-five, forty-five, fifty-five, sixty-five, and eighty-five?

How to create your life vision? Finding your purpose in life will help you create your vision.

1. You should first identify what's important to you in life. What do you believe in? What do you want to see changed, or what is it you don't want to see changed?

2. Be creative. Now is not the time to be safe in your goal setting. Your life vision should be something far-fetched and hard to accomplish but it should make you excited, think outside the box.

3. Write out a vision statement for your life.

4. Write out an outline for the steps you intend to take to reach your finish line. Even if your vision seems so

far away, you should still be able to outline steps that will take you there.

Don't let yourself feel overwhelmed when creating a life vision. You can always change your plans, just get started. If you find that your goals and priorities have changed, you can always revisit and revise your vision at any time.

Exercise assignment: write a script six months from now in the present tense living the way you really want to live and earning the profits you really want to earn.

Go to www.iamlife888.com for more information and to schedule your free breakthrough call or by email at 888Iamlife@gmail.com.

CHAPTER 4

CHECK YOUR HABITS

Your habits show what thoughts need adjustments.

I want to talk to you about what's really going on. Have you set out to make some much-needed positive changes in your life and realized it was just so hard to stick to? You had good intentions and it may have even worked for just a little while although you were looking for lasting effects.

We tell ourselves we're going to change our eating habits, we're going to exercise more and be more active, we say we're going to stop smoking, stop drinking, maybe free ourselves from toxic relationships, going to make changes with whatever goals we come up with, and it always seems like it's just a matter of time before we're back to doing the same old thing.

There's a reason behind that and it is our program system. Let me explain what I mean by that. When we think, feel, and act in a particular way over a period of time, habits form, not only in our behavior but in our memory system too. Let's take a look into habits. Of course, there are good habits and bad habits, and we all have them. Breaking or changing habits can be tough, however, it can certainly be done. See a lot of times we attempt to change our habits from a conscious level and not at the subconscious level. The subconscious level is where all the action is.

Let's take a closer look into "habits." Once you get a better understanding of how habits are formed, you'll be able to change or replace any habit you desire.

The word *habit* means established disposition of the mind. A recurrent, often unconscious pattern of behavior that is acquired through frequent repetition

In order to live the life that we were created to live, that life that we desire deep down inside, the life that imagination takes us to, we must change some of our habits. Knowing how to break bad habits is worth its weight in gold.

Changing just one or two habits makes a huge difference. You shouldn't try to change more than one or two habits at once. It'll become too big, and you won't change any. However, if you pick just one or two habits to replace and stick with your plan until the new behavior becomes automatic, it will make a huge difference in your life. Remember, if you don't replace a bad habit with a good habit, you would most likely, automatically replace your bad habit with another bad habit.

Changing your habits changes your life. There are times we keep getting the same results over and over after all the effort we put into changing. Why is that? What is keeping us in that same place? It is called our paradigm.

You might ask what is a paradigm? Well, a paradigm is a mental program in your subconscious mind with almost exclusive control over your habitual behavior. No matter how hard you try, it is difficult to earn more, do more, and be more until you change your mental program.

Take a closer look into your mind and your paradigm. Know that your mind is an activity, not a thing. No one has ever seen the mind. The mind is separated into two categories, the conscious mind and the subconscious mind. It's the subconscious mind where all the work is done. The body is an instrument of the mind. Understanding this concept can help create a whole new life for yourself.

The conscious mind is your thinking mind. Thinking is the highest function we are capable of yet very few people think. Not only is a conscious mind our thinking mind, this part of our mind also becomes our educated mind and our intellect.

The conscious mind because we can think, we have the ability to choose, so we can accept or reject anything that comes our way. That's where our freedom really comes in. So if we reject something that comes our way we can originate something new.

The subconscious mind is our emotional mind, and it operates differently from the conscious mind. The subconscious mind must accept anything you give it, it cannot reject. The subconscious mind cannot determine the difference between what is real or what is imagined. If you can imagine something in your subconscious mind, it will be real.

So just to be clear on this, your conscious mind represents your thinking mind, educated mind, your intellect, and has the ability to choose, accept, reject, and originate.

Your subconscious mind represents your emotional mind, and it has the ability to only accept and cannot reject.

This is what we do today, we are open to social media, Netflix, podcasts, other people, and a conscious mind has been touched by all of this information, however, we have in our conscious mind the ability to think, we can accept or reject if we think about it. Most times we don't think, and we leave our minds wide open, and then it goes right into our subconscious mind, and we do that because of paradigms.

As infants, we were being inundated with all kinds of things, negative and positive. People think, *Oh, they don't know they're just babies.* Truth is, their subconscious mind is wide open. They may not know intellectually or consciously but the subconscious mind sucks it right up.

Now back to paradigms. Another way to look at paradigms is it is a multitude of ideas that have been dumped into your subconscious mind. It's been programmed since childhood. We have gathered an abundance of knowledge, covering numerous subjects. However, most of us have learned very little if anything at all about paradigms. Therefore, we frequently do not do what we already know how to do. We had superior knowledge with inferior results which equals confusion and frustration.

We all know brilliant people but yet they're getting poor results. Why is that? Results are caused by paradigm, nothing to do with how smart people are. It has everything to do with the paradigm, it's our program. We have been programmed by people we were around as a child and most likely we kept those kinds of people around throughout our adulthood. Now if you want to change your results you must change your paradigm. You cannot change results without changing your paradigm.

Here are a couple of ways to change a paradigm. Paradigms can be changed through repetition and elite-level coaching and emotional impact. Change the paradigm in the same manner that it was formed—through repetition of ideas. Expose yourself to a new idea over and over again with the goal of replacing an old belief or beliefs that are in your conscious mind.

Consciously choose a new belief that is aligned with the results you want and the habit that would lead you to those results.

Impress that idea by focusing on it, visualizing it, and repeating it with feeling on your subconscious mind repeatedly. Repetition is the key to changing your subconscious patterns.

You must also consciously and deliberately replace "bad" habits with good habits. Otherwise, you may form another bad habit to take the old bad habits place.

Also know that if you really want to change your life, it is important to be around people with similar mindsets.

Change paradigms one idea at a time. The results always tell you what's in your paradigm. Write out on paper what you want. Repetition is needed as well as getting into action right away. It's said that 95 percent of success is the mindset and 5 percent is strategy. Repetition is your best friend in changing your paradigm. Start acting like the person you want to be, now. The little things compound over time is what create results.

Ralph Waldo Emerson said, "Do the thing, and you shall have the power."

Go to www.iamlife888.com for more information and to schedule your free breakthrough call or by email at <u>888Iamlife@</u> <u>gmail.com</u>.

CHAPTER 5

CHECK YOUR ATTITUDE

Making and maintaining attitude shifts
when needed is important in life.

Our attitude is the environment we carry with us during the day. It proclaims to the world what we think of ourselves and indicates the sort of person we have made up our minds to be. It is the person we will become. How's your attitude today? (Bob Proctor)

One of the most important steps you can take toward achieving your greatest potential in life is to learn to monitor your attitude. It takes a positive attitude to achieve positive results. Attitude governs the way you perceive the world, and the way the world perceives you.

We all have a choice on how we handle things that come up and life. Each of us experience physical and emotional pain, hard times, hurt feelings, and so on. The key is to realize it's not what happens to you that matters; it's how you choose to respond.

An enthusiastic attitude is nothing more than faith in action. Be cheerful, positive, and determined—you will go far. The person with the attitude that he can't do something is most often correct. The person who does believe they can do something, maybe not on the first try, but his attitude gives him the confidence to continue to try until he has accomplished his goal. Successful people come in all ages, shapes, sizes, and colors, but they all have one thing in common, a winning attitude.

You live simultaneously in three planes of understanding. You have an intellect, you have an emotional mind, and you have a physical body. Attitude is the composite of the thoughts in the intellect, the feelings in the subconscious, and the actions of the physical body. It's the composite of all three. (Bob Proctor)

Here are a few simple thoughts that can help you switch your attitude:

- Instead of saying "I can't," say "I can."
- Instead of saying "impossible," say "possible."
- Instead of saying "I'm not," say "I am."
- Instead of saying "this is bad," say "this is good.".
- Instead of saying "But what if this doesn't work?" say "What if this does work?"

Earl Nightingale gives a few points to keep in mind.

1. It is our attitude at the beginning of a task, which more than anything else, will affect its successful outcome.

2. It is our attitude towards life that determines life's attitude towards us.

3. We are interdependent. It is impossible to succeed without others, and it is our attitude towards others that will determine their attitude towards us.

4. Before a person can achieve the kind of life he wants, he must first become that kind of individual. He must act, think, talk, walk, and conduct himself in all affairs as if he is already the individual he wishes to become.

5. The higher you go in any organization of value, the better will be the attitude you will find.

6. Your mind can hold only one thought at a time. So since not much good comes out of negative thoughts, you might as well think positive.

7. The deepest craving of human beings is to be needed, to feel important, and to be appreciated. Give it to them and they will return it to you.

8. Look for the best and new ideas.

9. Don't waste valuable time broadcasting personal problems. It most likely will not help you and it cannot help others.

10. Don't talk about your health unless it's good

11. Radiate the attitude of well-being, of confidence, of a person who knows where he's going. This will inspire those who are around you, and you'll find good things will start happening to you.

12. For the next thirty days, treat everyone you come in contact with as if they are the most important person on earth. If you can do this for thirty days, you can do this for a lifetime.

Don't let a negative attitude ruin your life. A negative attitude will almost guarantee that life will be more difficult and less fulfilling than it should be. Attitude is everything, for better or worse. The way you perceive and explain the world has a powerful effect on the results you obtain. A pessimistic outlook will adversely affect your health, relationships, and professional growth.

What are some indications of a negative attitude? How does a negative attitude develop?

So according to the mental health experts, negative people often have a hard time recognizing these behaviors in themselves. A few signs have been provided to help you become aware of any necessary attitude adjustments that may be needed.

1. Social media stresses you out if when you get on Facebook, Twitter, or Instagram and your temperature rises and your blood boils, because you are seeing the good times that other people are having, you may be a bit too negative.

2. You think you're too old for everything. Sure, there are some things that we grow out of such as hanging out all night with the thirty-year-old, and we're sixty-five. However, if the phrase "I'm too old for that" comes out of your vocabulary frequently, you may need to check your negativity.

3. The past dictates your future, professionals point out that negative people tend to limit their options to

whatever they have done in the past rather than open-ing their minds to the range of possibilities available to them today.

4. To avoid failing, you'd rather not try. Most people get nervous about the possibilities that come with putting in effort or trying something new. However, if you're not even willing to try, then that is something to be worried about. Most times the refusal to try something different to bring positive change in our lives is usually rooted in fear. Taking a closer look into the root of the fear would also be helpful.

5. You can't deviate from your routine, it's one thing to have a routine you like; it's another thing to be so firmly stuck in that it makes you uncomfortable to veer from your daily script. For instance, a detour was set in place on your way home from work and instead of looking at it as an opportunity to explore new areas or maybe even find a new coffee shop on the way home you decided to get upset which blinded you from noticing any new possibilities.

6. You procrastinate. When you think of procrastination you may not relate it to how negative or positive it can be but according to studies, procrastination is often rooted in a deep sense of self-doubt, which is certainly negative.

How does a negative attitude develop?

A bad attitude typically begins with an expectation of yourself or others. You want to please yourself or others, so you establish unrealistic expectations. When you fail to meet an unrealistic expectation, it will create a bad attitude and a negative environment. You need to accept that there's no perfect condition.

Below are a few simple ways to build a positive attitude:

1. Listen to good music with positive messages in it.
2. Don't watch television passively.
3. Don't do anything passively.
4. Be aware of negativity.
5. Make time to be alone.

6. Exercise.

7. Take time to do the things you enjoy.

8. Find ways to measure your progress, and then measure it.

9. Smile.

10. Have a purpose.

11. Change your thoughts.

12. Focus on the good.

13. Stop expecting life to be easy.

14. Visualize.

15. Limit your complaints.

16. Watch your words.

17. Use the power of humor.

18. Use gratitude to improve your attitude.

19. Give up on having an attitude of entitlement.

20. Seek out others with a positive attitude.

In conclusion, remember the statement made by John Mitchell, "Our attitude towards life determines life's attitude toward us."

Now Let's make a conscious decision to have a great attitude towards life.

Go to www.iamlife888.com for more information and to schedule your free breakthrough call or by email at <u>888Iamlife@</u> <u>gmail.com</u>.

CHAPTER 6

LETTING GO

In order to take hold of the life you want you

have to let go of the life you have.

Many of us have the tendency of holding on to things such as bitterness, hatred, resentment, hurt, anger, abuse, feelings of retaliation, disappointment, fear and so on. Holding onto such things serves as no benefit to us obtaining the life that we were created to have. Honestly, a lot of people are holding onto things from their past that they are not aware they're still holding onto.

Living in the past causes negative thoughts that not only affect your mind but also your health. They can lead to stress, anxiety, depression, insomnia, obesity, and anorexia. You feel tired all the time and you are not able to stay productive at work and enjoy all those little happy things life offers you.

If you don't let go of the past and make peace with it, it will haunt you for a lifetime. That negative energy will weigh you down. It will deter you and hinder you from leading a life of fulfillment and achievement. Although you may not think it will.

"Holding on to the past prevents you from realizing your future, hopes, and dreams. So quit looking back and press your way forward for the prize that awaits you" (Yvonne L. Wilson).

God wants the best for you.

Paul explains to us, "Brethren, I count not myself to have apprehended: but this one thing I do, forgetting those things which are behind, and reaching forth unto those things, which are before. I press toward the mark for the prize of the high calling of God in Christ Jesus" (Philippians 3:13–14).

The past cannot be changed, forgotten, edited, or erased; it can only be accepted. Don't lose your present to your past. Let us, therefore, quit looking back and press our way forward for the prize that awaits us in Christ. Forgive yourself! Forgive others! For your future awaits you.

Benefits of Letting Go

Notice the phrase "benefits of letting go." Letting go is a process that takes time. But the sooner you move through the process of letting go of what is hurting you, the sooner you'll be living in your better days.

1. You will learn to love yourself first.

2. You will grow closer to your destiny.

3. You will naturally attract what you need. "Abundance is a process of letting go; that which is empty can receive" (Bryant H. McGill).

4. You will realize a new positive version of yourself. "I use memories, but I will not allow memories to use me" (Deepak Chopra).

5. You will make room for the new. "Some changes look negative on the surface, but you will soon realize that

space is being created in your life for something new to emerge" (Eckhart Tolle).

6. You will handle obstacles with grace. "The past should be a learning experience not an everlasting punishment. What's done is done" (Unknown).

7. You will experience a new sense of freedom.

The benefit of experiencing a new sense of freedom, reminds me of a story I once heard. Told by James McNeil, he mentioned that he had learned of a tropical island that had lots of monkeys there, it was explained to him how they caught monkeys. They said they would cut holes into coconuts just small enough for the monkey to slide his hand in, and on the other side of the hole was a rope or string-like material set up so as the monkey reached his hand inside, they could pull that string and it would tighten up to hold onto the monkey's wrists. That's how they caught the monkeys.

Now to explain further, the villagers did a test and realize even if they weren't on the other end to pull the string, the monkeys would still be there stuck in the coconut. The reason for this is because once the monkey put his hand in the hole, reaching into the coconut, he grabbed what was inside therefore his hand was in a fist. While his hand was in a fist, the monkey was unable to move his hand out of the hole. The hole wasn't made big enough for a fist to come through and once the monkey grabbed onto the substance that was inside the coconut, he wouldn't let it go. He would not loosen up his hold, his grip and because he chose to hold on, he wasn't able to free himself.

See, if the monkey had chosen to let go of what he was holding onto, he would have experienced freedom. Like so many of us, holding onto hurt, pain, resentment, and so many other things of the past, we are unable to experience the freedom that we should be living in. I strongly urge you to let it go so you can move forward.

Let's take driving a vehicle, for instance—there's a reason why the rearview mirror is smaller than the windshield. The rearview mirror is not made to place all focus on. The rearview mirror is meant for occasional glances while the windshield was created to place all your focus on. In order to move forward, you have to look forward. Tell me, how far ahead could you safely get if you keep your focus on the rearview mirror?

Let the past be just that, the past. Free yourself from what's behind you. Look at what's ahead of you and move forward. There's a bright future ahead, waiting for you to show up.

Now that you know the importance and benefits of letting go, let's talk about how to let go.

Here are just a few ways that can help you put into practice letting go of what's behind you:

1. *Make it a habit to notice and focus on what's good in your life.* It serves you well to focus on what's good in your life and leaves little to no time thinking about what's not. The more you focus on what's good, the more energy you feed into that good and the more good you'll receive.

2. *Create a positive mantra to counter the painful thoughts.* How you speak to yourself will either move you forward or hold you back. Having a positive mantra to

say to yourself while in an emotional state can help reframe your thoughts.

3. *Create physical distance.* It is not unreasonable to distance yourself from situations or people who are causing you grief.

4. *Surround yourself with people who fill you up.* We are not created to live life alone. However, it's very important to be mindful of the type of people you are around. Being around positive people who tend to fill you up is certainly recommended.

5. *Seek professional help.* Sometimes it's necessary to seek out a professional to help you sort through your thoughts and feelings in order to be honest with yourself so you can address the situation and make the necessary changes needed to let go and move forward.

6. *Forgive.* Give yourself permission to forgive, whether it's directed to someone else or to yourself. Forgiveness is not for others, it's for you. With or without an apology, forgiveness is vital to the healing process because it allows you to let go of the anger, guilt, shame, sad-

ness, or any other feelings you may be experiencing that's keeping you from moving on.

Most people find it difficult to let go of the past because they don't appreciate their present. Reframing our relationships with our past requires us to stop thinking of how things should be and accept them for what there are.

Here's what Gods' Word has to say about letting go of the past:

> Forget what happened long ago! Don't think about the past. I am creating something new. There it is! Do you see it? I have put roads in deserts, streams in thirsty lands. (Isaiah 43:18–19 CEV)

> But Jesus said to him, "No one, having put his hand to the plow, and looking back, is fit for the kingdom of God." (Luke 9:62)

Let all bitterness and wrath and anger and clamor and slander be put away from you, along with all malice. Be kind to one another, tenderhearted, forgiving one another, as God in Christ forgave you. (Ephesians 4:31–32)

Let your eyes look straight ahead; fix your gaze directly before you. (Proverbs 4:25)

Go to www.iamlife888.com for more information and to schedule your free breakthrough call or by email at 888Iamlife@gmail.com.

CHAPTER 7

MAKE THE COMMITMENT

Commit to yourself, your goals, and your purpose.

Learn to make yourself a priority and put you first. We often make it a habit to put others and their needs ahead of our own. That stops right here, right now. It's time to make a commitment to ourselves, our goals and dreams, and our purpose. You deserve it. You owe it to yourself to love yourself, think highly of yourself, believe in yourself, and to commit to your personal development by investing in yourself. Bet on you like you bet on everyone else. "You have greatness in you," as Les Brown often says, so don't let fear and excuses keep you from letting your greatness shine through. Trust the process.

Meyer (2002) defines commitment to change as a force (mindset) that binds an individual to a course of action deemed necessary for the successful implementation of a change initiative. This mindset can reflect a desire to provide support for the change based on a belief in its inherent benefits.

See after everything we've been through leading up to the changes, we've made to better serve ourselves and those around us, times of doubt will try to enter our minds. We'll start to wonder if we're doing the right thing, did we make the right choices and decisions, nothing seems to be changing fast enough and so on. Trust me, not all change happens overnight.

Remember earlier we talked about treating ourselves as if we were the garden, and the information we take in is like seeds being planted. Nothing comes up overnight except weeds and with that being said, some of the ideas and beliefs that we are currently changing, they have been deposited into our lives (soil) over long periods of time, and therefore, their roots run very deep.

In the earlier chapters, we've discussed the similarities of planting a seed in the ground and us putting good information in our hearts. You clear all mess away from the area in which you plan to plant. You dig a hole deep enough. You drop the seed in and cover it back up with the soil. You water it and make sure proper sunlight is provided and to make certain the environment is set to cause the seed to germinate.

Our lives may also seem (much like the seeds) to experience a state of dormancy, which is a delay in germination until conditions are right for survival and growth. That is why we must stay committed to keeping our ground. Keep trash out, weeds included, and continue with nurturing ourselves with what's needed and making sure our environment remains right for growth. Keep ourselves encouraged, stay away from drama and negativity, bitterness, anger, fear, and other toxicity. Continue with your daily affirmations and mind set books and motivational and self-empowering videos, etc.

Just because you can't see what's going on underground doesn't mean germination isn't taking place.

> Like a farmer who scatters seed on the ground. Night and day, while he's asleep or awake, the seed sprouts and grows, but he does not understand how it happens. The earth produces the crops on its own. First a leaf blade pushes through, then the heads of wheat are formed, and finally the grain ripens. And as soon as the grain is ready, the farmer comes and harvests it with a sickle, for the harvest time has come. (Mark 4:26–29 NLT)

It takes time and consistency to remove and replace. It takes commitment and dedication to continue to do what's necessary to create the changes we want to see take place in our lives (new fruit). It's not a one-shot deal. Change often is subtle. First the blade, then the ear, and after that the full corn in the ear. You'll notice things you used to do that served no purpose for a positive impact on your life are no longer things you want to do. You'll find yourself interested in doing things you may not have ever been interested in before, however, these newfound interests are things that help get you closer to your destiny. Commit to learning new things that will bring you closer to your goals and your dreams. Continue to replace the negative stuff that's in your life with positive things that will serve to be beneficial in your life. No one said it was ever going to be easy, but it certainly is or will be worth it. One foot in front of the other, continue to walk forward

Don't be so quick to look for secrets and shortcuts, you'll miss out on the hard work and dedication required to achieve great success. The most successful people are committed to doing the hard work, serving their purpose, and prioritizing their well-being first.

To live a life you're proud of, one full of meaning and purpose, you need to build it for yourself. No one can hand it to you, nor will they. Holding yourself accountable requires you to let go of your victim mindset, heal from your trauma, and utilize your adversities as a source of growth.

Success in life is not based on merit alone. It requires hard work, strategy, personal sacrifices, and extreme focus. We all have choices to make. Those that achieve their goals are more willing to make and stick to the harder ones.

We need to continue to remind ourselves what it is we want and why we want it. If you discover what you thought you wanted isn't really what you want, it's okay to change that and start focusing on what it is you really do want. Change isn't always easy, however, it's often something you're happy you did in the long run.

Reflect on whether or not your behaviors align with your life's mission and purpose. Alignment requires minimizing external forces, eliminating distractions, and making sacrifices to focus on what you truly need. Develop uncompromisable discipline.

At times you may feel a sense of loneliness due to the removal of all the mess you've cut out from your life. There are certain people you have limited yourself to be around now,

TV shows you may not watch anymore, and maybe you've cut down how much news you're taking in.

Making these changes in my life did me wonders. Honestly, there's been times I've confused the strong sense of peace I now had in my life as loneliness. I had so much peace in me that I didn't know what to do with myself. Making it a point to find like-minded individuals became a saving grace for me. This is not a "do it alone" journey. We all need support. Find groups and communities where you can encourage and support each other.

> The only limit to your impact is your imagination and commitment. (Anthony Robbins)

> Unless commitment is made, there are only promises and hopes...but no plans. (Peter F. Drucker)

The quality of a persons' life is in direct proportion to their commitment to excellence, regardless of their chosen field of endeavor. (Vince Lombardi)

Desire is the key to motivation, but it's determination and commitment to an unrelenting pursuit of your goal—a commitment to excellence—that will enable you to attain the success you seek. (Mario Andretti)

Great changes may not happen right away, but with effort even the difficult may become easy. (Bill Blackman)

Anyone can dabble, but once you've made that commitment, your blood has that particular thing in it, and it's very hard for people to stop you. (Bill Cosby)

There's a difference between interest and commitment. When you're interested in doing something, you do it only when circumstances permit. When you're committed to something, you accept no excuses, only results. (Art Turock)

Let us not become weary in doing good, for at the proper time we will reap a harvest if we do not give up. (Galatians 6:9)

Brothers and sisters, I do not consider myself yet to have taken hold of it. But one thing I do: Forgetting what is behind and straining toward what is ahead. (Philippians 3:13)

Commit to the Lord whatever you do, and he will establish your plans. (Proverbs 16:3)

I can do all things through Christ who strengthens me. (Philippians 4:13)

I have fought the good fight, I have finished the race, I have kept the faith. (2 Timothy 4:7)

Blessed is the man who remains steadfast under trial, for when he has stood the test he will receive the crown of life, which God has promised to those who love him. (James 1:12)

No discipline seems pleasant at the time, but painful. Later on, however, it produces a harvest of righteousness and peace for those who have been trained by it. (Hebrews 12:11)

"And God blessed them. And God said to them, 'Be fruitful, and multiply, and replenish the earth...'" (Genesis 1:28).

Right here in this verse, God has blessed us from the beginning, and he has commanded us to be fruitful and to multiply. We need to have faith in the blessing that God has bestowed on our lives and act on it and commit to it. We all have something great inside waiting for us to unleash it. So let's commit to ourselves, our goals, and dreams, and live the life we were created to live. Let's create and live our life of excellence right now. Someone is waiting for you to show up. Stay focused and committed and remember God has already blessed you for such a time as this. All you need to do is take a step forward. I'll see you on the other side of your destiny.

Go to www.iamlife888.com for more information and to schedule your free breakthrough call or by email at 888Iamlife@gmail.com.

ABOUT THE AUTHOR

Nicole is not just a beautiful woman on the outside but also a beautiful woman from within. She and her sister were raised in church from early on and eventually became pastor's kids. Nicole had an adventurous and outgoing personality, which soon led to her experimenting with things outside the church. Nicole found herself hanging around people she had no business hanging around and certainly doing things she wasn't familiar within the household or environment she grew up in. She came from church and private schools straight to being introduced to the lifestyle of using and selling drugs.

At the age of twenty-four, Nicole cried out to God for help in delivering her from that rabbit hole she went down, and now God has led her to coaching and teaching others how to claim the life God has set out for them. Nicole's presence brightens up any room she enters. Her sense of humor will have you laughing in no time and forgetting any issues you may have had. Nicole is said to be delightful and certainly spirited. She will help anyone in need whether she knows you or not. She's been in the field of helping others for the majority of her life. God has continued to smile on Nicole, and His light clearly shines bright right through her. Nicole's excitement for God is truly visible, and she is passionate about helping others who want change make a change and break through all barriers to go further than they have imagined. Nicole encourages you to dream big and shows you the steps to take to accomplish your goals. Nicole has certainly been kept for such a time as this.

Go to www.iamlife888.com for more information and to schedule your free breakthrough call or by email at 888Iamlife@gmail.com.

CPSIA information can be obtained
at www.ICGtesting.com
Printed in the USA
BVHW081731120123
656162BV00003B/288